AND THIS IS LOVE

A Spiritual Guide

by
EVANGELIST JOHN DYE

Order this book online at www.trafford.com
or email orders@trafford.com

Most Trafford titles are also available at major online book retailers.

Note for Librarians: A cataloguing record for this book is available from Library and Archives Canada at www.collectionscanada.ca/amicus/index-e.html

Printed in Victoria, BC, Canada.

ISBN: 9781-4120-9374-3 (soft cover)
ISBN: 9781-4251-9799-5 (eBook)

We at Trafford believe that it is the responsibility of us all, as both individuals and corporations, to make choices that are environmentally and socially sound. You, in turn, are supporting this responsible conduct each time you purchase a Trafford book, or make use of our publishing services. To find out how you are helping, please visit www.trafford.com/responsiblepublishing.html

Our mission is to efficiently provide the world's finest, most comprehensive book publishing service, enabling every author to experience success. To find out how to publish your book, your way, and have it available worldwide, visit us online at www.trafford.com

 **Trafford** PUBLISHING® www.trafford.com

North America & international
toll-free: 1 888 232 4444 (USA & Canada)
phone: 250 383 6864 ♦ fax: 250 383 6804 ♦ email: info@trafford.com

The United Kingdom & Europe
phone: +44 (0)1865 487 395 ♦ local rate: 0845 230 9601
facsimile: +44 (0)1865 481 507 ♦ email: info.uk@trafford.com

10 9 8 7 6 5 4 3 2 1

CONTENTS

Note: Asterisks (*) represent "footnotes" in alphabetical order

INTRODUCTION

This book was written not to replace your Holy Bible, but it was written to be in agreement with it. And to spark the spirits fire of the individual reading this book. So that he or she might have a deeper understanding into the truth of God's word (in love).

By Author:
John T. Dye Jr.
(Man of God)

CHAPTER ONE

Spiritual Foundation of Life

WALKING WITH GOD

God has put in order a foundation of life that no man can change.

God
Men (who love God)
Women who love (men who love God)
And Children who love (parents who love God)

This is called: The blessed hope!

Footnotes:

Extras:
Ex 19:5-6
Dt 4:1-40
Dt 6:1-25,
1Cor. 2:6-16
1Cor. 7:15-20,39
1Cor. 9:5-6
1Cor. 11:7-12
1Cor. 13:1-13
1Pe 3:1-22
2Pe 1:3-4
2Pe 1:19-21,
1Tim 2:1-15

LIVING TO PLEASE GOD

The blessed hope (Holy marriage) is a state of blessedness in which all the members of the family are born again because God wants to create a people for himself (set apart to be like God; loyal, faithful, and Holy).

God has said; "I am Holy even so you be Holy."* So the parents should be born again with the children being train in the lord. Then everyone will be able to enter the good life as well as the kingdom of heaven; also your eyes can see a blessing and the kingdom of heaven. Then you will be able to hear Gods voice and walk in spirit and truth.

And this is love as found in scriptures as the truth to the Fathers glory, in the Son, and the Holy Spirit!*

Footnotes:
    a. Lev. 19:1-4
    b. Mt. 28:18-20

Extras:
    Ex. 19:3-8
    Ex. 31:12-13
    Jn. 3:1-21
    Jn. 4:23-24
    Act. 2:40-41

VICTORY

God has predestined you and the family for glory before the creation of the world.*

The promise is for you and your children and for all who are far off; whom the Lord our God will call.*

Jesus said: "My family are those who do the will of my father in heaven."*

Footnotes:
   a. Eph. 1:5,11
   b. Ac. 2:39
   c. Mt. 12:48-50

CHAPTER TWO

In the Beginning

CREATION

In the beginning God created the heavens and the earth and everything found in them. And God said: "That it was good!"

Then God said: "Let us create man in our image" (he created man a little lower than the angels) so God made them male and female. God blessed them and said, "Be fruitful and multiply; be careful to take care of the earth and overcome it."

Footnotes:
   Ge. 1:1-28

Extras:
   Ge. 12:1-8

PERFECT PEACE

Then God rested from all his work and looked at what he had created, and it was very good! (Perfect)**

God expected the man of God, and woman of man, to raise Godly offspring. And continue a legacy of holiness on earth. (Heaven on earth)

Footnotes:
   a. Ge. 2:1-3
   b. Ge. 1:31

Extras:
   Separate – Ge. 12:1-8
   Vision – Ge. 13:14-18,
   Trust – Ge. 26:2-6
   Meditate – Ge. 28:10-14
   Mediator – Ac. 3:17-26
   Spiritual – Ac. 17:24-34
   Faith – Ro. 4:16-25

CHAPTER THREE

Paradise

HOLY MARRIAGE

Now that God has laid out the heavens and earth in relationship to one another according to his will and good pleasure. Paradise is truly a blessed state to remain in because you're in Gods presence at all times.

Therefore God blessed the marriage:

God

Men (who love God)

Women who love (men who love God)

And children who love (parents who love God)

This three-strand cord is not easily broken.* What God has joined together let no man separate* (Holy marriage), especially, two believers of holiness training their children to understand the love of God.

As we move on from here we see further evidence of Gods order and God holding everyone accountable to keeping the order!*

Footnotes:
    a. Eccl. 4:12
    b. Mt. 19:4-6
    c. Ge. 3:9,13,17

GOD GIVEN AUTHORITY

So God said, that he had created this perfect life style called "paradise", but there was no one to take care of it. So he put man in charge of it (to take care of it and work it) to make it fruitful.*

And God said, "To the man in the garden of paradise, of every tree here you may freely eat, but of the tree of the knowledge of good and evil you must not eat, for the day you eat of this tree you will surely die!*

Footnotes:
 a. Ge. 2:4-8
 b. Ge. 2:16-17

Extras:
 Ge. 15:1

OBEDIENCE

So at this point, we see God has given us some commands to follow let us point out these commands.

- First: God commands us to raise children in the Lord. (Godly offspring)*

- Second: God commands us to take care of what he has given us and to take care of what he has given us to live on (the earth and the blessings of paradise).*

- Third: God commands us to be content with what he has provided and not to seek our own understanding, but rely on God. (Faith)**

Footnotes:
    a. Pr. 22:6
    b. Ge. 1:28
    c. Phil. 4:12
    d. Heb. 11:1

Extras:
    Purpose – 1Cor. 9:24-27
    Covenant – Ge. 17:1-14
    Teacher – Lk 6:39-40

WORKING FOR GOD

Now God trusts the man, he put in charge because God has given the man his spirit. When God breathed into his nostrils the breath of life. (That is truly life to live with God in his presence). Then man became a living being.*

Since man has the Holy Spirit, God allows the man to name everything and whatever the man named it that was its name!*

Footnotes:
    a. Ge. 2:7
    b. Ge. 2:19

A HELP MATE

And God said, "It's not good for man to be alone." (Now it's important to note that up to this point the man of God is faithfully doing everything just as God has commanded him).

So God decides to make him a woman and God brings the woman to him to see what the man would name her. The man names her woman/ bone of his bone. (Meaning one flesh)*

Note: God did not name the woman (The man did)!

At this point, we see God did not go behind the man's back and re-name anything, that's not God's character to double cross. God does not lie or change his order of life.

So God tells the couple to move away from there kinfolks and the two have in deed become one flesh in the unity of love in paradise.*

Footnotes:
    a. Ge. 2:18-24
    b. Ge 2:24

CHAPTER FOUR

Overview

GOD'S FOUNDATION OF LIFE

So we see God has established his foundation of life in paradise for good living.

God as the head of the marriage namely (man),

Man as the head of the (woman),

And parents as the head of the (children) mainly woman.*

One: We see man will be blessed, if he listens to God.*

Two: Woman will be blessed, if she listens to her man of God. (Husband)*

Three: Children will live long and be blessed, if they obey their (Parents).*

Footnotes:
   a. 1Tim. 3:1-15
   b. Ge. 3:17
   c. 1Tim. 2:11-15
   d. Eph. 6:1-4

Extras:
   Col. 3:20
   1Tim. 4:1-16
   2Tim. 3:16-17
   Tit. 2:1-15
   Heb. 5:11-14
   Heb. 12:7-15

CHAPTER FIVE

Rebellion in Heaven

Rebellion in Heaven

THE REASON

Now here is where the problem comes in. You know, when everything is going good something has to happen! (There is a reason for this.)

The reason is about the time God put everything in order on earth, which occupied most of his time because God does things right the first time.

God left three angels in charge of heaven. (Arc-angels)**

One: Michael – in charge of the army of God. (Faithful)*

Two: Gabriel – in charge of the messages of God. (Diligent)*

Three: Lucifer – in charge of the praises of God. (Loyalty)*

The problem is Lucifer got tired, envious, jealous, proud, arrogant, selfish, rebellious, and rude. Lucifer did not want to be loyal anymore, so Lucifer convinced a group of angels to rebel against heaven and Gods commands.*

Footnotes:
a. Ge. 2:1-3
b. Rev. Ch. 12
c. Rev. 12: 7-8
d. Dan. 8: 15-19
e. Isa. 14: 12-23
f. Rev. 12: 3,4,7-9

Extras:
Michael – Jude 9, Dan. 10:13,21, Dan. 12:1
Gabriel – Dan. 9:20-23, Lk. 1:11-20, Lk. 1: 26-38
Lucifer – Job 1: 6, Zec. 3: 2, Mt. 16: 23

DECEIVER PART ONE

To be truthful, Lucifer was not carrying out half of Gods commands and Lucifer knew that God was going to eventually check on him. Sooner or later (it was just a matter of time).*

God was going to find out Lucifer had not kept his word. And Lucifer was going to be out of heaven for lying to God continuously.*

Lucifer did not want to go alone (because misery loves company). So before any one could find out what he was up too, Lucifer deceived some other angels and convinced them God was not worthy to be praised, or to receive the glory and honor do him.*

Footnotes:
> a. Pr. 15:3
> b. Rev. 12:3,4,7-9
> c. Rev. 12:7-9

Extras:
> Mk. 4:15
> 2Cor. 11:14
> Rev. 12:9
> Rev. 20:2,7

TRIAL

God did get around to checking on his kingdom, (heaven and the angels) only to find out, that one of his angels had been mocking him, lazy, and tricking all the other angels into disobedience.*

Then God called for Michael and Gabriel top angels in heaven (to be fair and establish the facts by two or three witnesses.)*

God wanted to know, what should be done to Lucifer for the rebellion he has caused?

Footnotes:
    a. Dt. 17: 2-5
    b. Dt. 17: 6-7

VERDICT

There was only one conclusion to banish Lucifer from heaven, so no other angel would learn his ways.

So God commanded Michael to take an army of angels and put heaven back in order. Do what ever it takes, but restore order and glory to heaven.**

Footnotes:
   a. Dt. 17:2-4
   b. Rev. 12:7-9

Rebellion in Heaven

WAR IN HEAVEN

Michael and his angels fought against Lucifer and his angels. The result: Lucifer and his angels lost their place in heaven and they were hurled down to the earth.

Gabriel speaks, "Woe to you people on earth because Lucifer (now called Satan because of his rebellious and un-loyal nature) has been cast down around you. Satan is full of fury because he knows that his time is short."*

Footnotes:
    a. Rev. 12:12

CHAPTER SIX

False Prophet

False Prophet

SATAN'S VIEW

God knew that Satan would attempt to deceive his creation. Satan would try to twist the word of God around (because Satan was around God everyday).

Therefore Satan says, that's not what God meant. He tells people God is not worthy to be praised everyday. Satan tells them to take time to glorify yourselves and have fun. (That's what God meant)

Satan says, I know because I used to be with God.**

Footnotes:
    a. Rev.12: 7-9,12,17
    b. Isa.14: 12-23

False Prophet

UNGODLY VIEW

People should ask the Question why isn't (Satan) with God now, but people simply go along with Satan's lies because they want to be independent.

They (people) want to be their own God. People want power, money, glory, and to be in control of their own lives.*

Notice: I did not say (self-control). There is a real difference as you will soon see!

Footnotes:
    a. 2 Tim. 3: 1-5

False Prophet

TEMPTATION

Back to earth, paradise, and the frustration, that comes with the Devil or Satan being allowed to tempt the people of God.*

The reason: God has put heaven in order!

Now everybody who enters heaven must first be tested to see, if their faithful to God or choose Satan and his followers.*

Note: Satan is also called the Devil.*

We will switch names here to (Devil).

At this point, we are giving the woman the benefit of not knowing the difference because the enemy will change names and masquerade as an angel of light.*

The woman not knowing the difference, that both names have the same meaning.

(It's still the ancient serpent called the devil or Satan)

That attempts to lead the whole world astray.*

As the woman was roaming through the garden of paradise, she met the Devil and the Devil asked her. What were the rules for Paradise?*

So the woman told the Devil. We may eat from any tree in the garden, but not from the tree in the middle of the garden and you must not touch it or you will die.

At this point, we see some things going on here. I don't believe the woman sounded to convincing to the Devil because keep in mind the Devil knows the word too!*

The Devil knew, that the woman left out the word (free), she add the word (touch), and she made it sound as if they (might die) not surely die!*

Note: How important it is to study God's word as a family.

Footnotes:
    a. Job 1: 6-12
    b. Dt. 30: 19-20
    c. Rev. 12:12
    d. 2Cor. 11: 14
    e. Rev. 12: 9

Extras: Satan schemes/ tricks – 2 Cor. 2: 11, Eph. 6: 10-12
    f. Ge. 3: 1
    g. Mt. 4: 1-11
    h. Ge. 3: 2-4

Extras: written history – Hab. 2: 2-4, 1 Cor. 10: 1-13, Ps. 1: 1-3

False Prophet

IMPORTANCE OF KNOWING GOD'S WORD

The Devil knew from conversations with the woman, that she did not run away immediately or say ask (my husband) because he knows the word better than me!*

One: that's why God gave the woman a man of God. The man is the spiritual head of the family. The man is commanded to study the scriptures daily and to mediate on them day and night.**

Two: God's word tells us to cast down every imagination that sets itself up against the kingdom of heaven or paradise on earth.*

Third: God tells us not to lean to our own understanding and knowledge because it puffs up our mind and puts us in danger of falling from glory. (The good life)*

Footnotes:
a. Eph. 5: 22-28 / *Extras:* 1Cor. 14: 33-38, Ge. 39: 9-12
b. 1Cor. 11: 1-3
c. Ps. 1: 2
d. 2Cor. 10: 3-8
e. 1Cor. 8: 1

False Prophet

DISOBEDIENCE

So the woman did eat from the forbidden tree and she gave some to her husband. I'm convinced (this was not the first time) she had ate from this tree and then deceived and lead her husband into sin.

(More than likely by her lying to him as the devil had lied to her.)*

We see this same sinful nature (way too often) in our society today to dismiss, what I'm saying.

D.N.A evidence has proven this to be true.*

Note: In this section, there is a repeat performance just as Satan had tried to deceive God earlier in heaven by not keeping his word or doing his job. (Praising God)

Satan does it again, but this time it's the woman on earth. The Devil is deceiving and teaching deceit too.*

The Devil did not go to the (man of God) first. He used the weaker mate. (Woman)

Footnotes:
   a. Ge. 3: 6 / *Extras*: Ge. 39: 6-12
   b. Ge. 3: 17 / *Extras*: 1Ki. 11: 1-4,7-9, Eph. 5: 22-24, Pr 31: 1-3
   c. Ge. 3: 13
   d. 1Pe. 3: 7 / *Extras*: 1Tim. 2: 14, 2Cor. 11: 3

CHAPTER SEVEN

The Results of Sin

DECEIVER PART TWO

The immediate result of sin is to deceive others by lying because you know the truth is going to come out. (Sooner or later)*

So people try to hide from one another, but the problem is you can't hide from God. God sees all things even the hidden things or those things done in the dark.*

Then God did come and ask for the man in charge.*

Footnotes:
   a. Ge. 3: 11-13 / *Extras*: Jer. 5: 1-3, Jer. 9: 3-9
   b. Heb. 4: 13
   c. Ge. 3: 9

The Results of Sin

THE BLAME GAME

So immediately the blame game starts and God goes down through his chain of command. (Godly order)
- Man of God first
- Woman of man second
- And eventually the serpent. (Devil / Satan)*

God also tells them the effect sin and deceit will have on their future children. (Turmoil and hostility)*

Note: That same turmoil and hostility are found in many books of the bible and families today.*

Godly order:
> God
> Man of God
> Woman of (Godly man)
> Children of (Godly parents)
> Satan (the tempter)

At this point, God still does not change the rules. God puts them away from the tree of immortality or life for now!*

Note: The man of God fell to the peer pressure from the world around him. (Instead of maintaining his testimony and protecting what God had gave him by calling on God first)*

- No weapon formed against you shall prosper.*
- If God is for us who can be against us.*
- My God will deliver me from all my troubles.*
- Everyone who calls on the name of the lord shall be saved.*

The Results of Sin

Note: The messages of God are to be understood and you are to hold on to his promises. (Patience)

Footnotes:
    a. Rev.12: 9
    b. Ge. 3: 9-15
    c. 2Sa. 12: 9-12
    d. Ge. 3: 22-24
    e. 1Cor. 10: 13 *Extras*: 1Cor. 15: 58, 1Cor. 16: 13
    f. Isa. 54: 17
    g. Ro. 8: 31
    h. Ps. 34: 17-19, *Extras*: Ps. 54: 7
    i. Ac. 2: 21, *Extras*: Joel 2: 32, Ro. 10: 13

Extras:
    Message – Isa. 53: 1, 2Cor. 2: 14-17
    Forgiveness – 2Cor. 2: 6-11, 2Cor. 7: 8-13
    Promises – Ac. 2: 39-41, 2Cor. 7: 1

GODLY DISCIPLINE

We see God tells the (man) because you listen to your wife, now life is going to be hard for you and your family. (Filled with confusion and hardships)*

God tells the (woman) because you listen to the serpent / Devil(This thing you've done!)* your desire is going to be for your husband. Your husband will rule over you and you will have much pain in your life. (Especially through your children)*

God tells the serpent (devil) from now on there will be (spiritual) war between the children of God and the children of the Devil with the (woman) caught in the middle of the mess!*

Note: War means no agreement between the children of God and the children of the Devil.*

Note: Now notice, I did not say man of God.
(I only said "man")

This is a worldly marriage (not a Holy marriage) because people are moving away from Gods presences (not toward God as we should.)

Footnotes:
    a. Ge. 3: 17
    b. Ge. 3: 13
    c. Ge. 3: 16
    d. Ge. 3: 15 / *Extras*: Eph. 6: 12, Rev. 12: 4-7
    e. 2Cor. 6: 16-17 / *Extras*: 1Jn. 2: 15-17

CHAPTER EIGHT

Worldly Marriage

LISTENING TO UNGODLINESS

It's not even good to be un-equally yoked with un-believers because of the danger of what we listen to on a daily basis. We must be conscious of it at all times.(Guard yourself spiritually)*

Half of our friends should not be un-believers and God forbid, if all of our friends are un-believers. (That's a person waiting to fall)*

Footnotes:
    a. 2Cor. 6: 14-18 / *Extras*: Phil. 4: 4-9
    b. 2 Pe. 2: 4-10

Worldly Marriage

FALLING AWAY FROM GOD

Now we see sin and rebellion takes us away from God and we do not live a life filled with all the good promises and the blessings of God ! (And not just that)

Sin turns people against one another, especially in marriages and families.

I would have to say; "The love of money, drug abuse, and adultery are the biggest contributors to a high divorce rate, family structure break down, and overall rebellion against Godliness !*

So we see why God warned us, that it's (not good) too:
- Lean to our own understanding.
- Trust in ourselves alone.
- Or become our own God.

But it's enough to be like God:
- Made in his image.
- Carrying out his commands.
- And understanding his ways.*

Footnotes:
    a. 2 Pe. 2: 7-8 / *Extras*: Ge. 39: 8-10, Jdg. 16: 16
    b. 1 Jn. 4: 5-6 / *Extras*: Pr. 3:5-6

CHAPTER NINE

A Lesson Learned

A Lesson Learned

SAY NO

We see the Devil can't wait to attack your marriage because he knows long lasting (Holy marriages) produce Godly offspring and Godly people.

Holy marriages are good examples of how, we should live on earth as it is in heaven.

Holy marriages encourage us all to do better and to become better people morally, physically, mentally, and spiritually.*

Footnotes:
   a. Ge. 39: 7-10 / *Extras*: 1Tim. 3: 12-13

A Lesson Learned

GOOD ADVICE

The wisdom of God

Morally: Because it protects our body from sickness and disease, if we obey Gods command of being united in one flesh. (Godly Marriage)*

Physically: Because we Exercise our body producing lovely physiques. (This is the temple of God)*

Mentally: Because our mind and affection ought to be on God, which gives us peace of mind about our daily lives. So we should think of praise worthy things. (Heavenly Things)*

Spiritually: Because it teaches us love for God, which binds everything else together with him (God) in this life and the life to come. (Eternity) And love for one another as well !*

Since all have fell short of the glory, that God predestined for us (the good life) in his presence. It only stands to reason, since many have been led astray. Now many must be called.*

Note: The question is asked, who, what, when, where, and why did the individual turn away from God.*

Footnotes:
    a. Ge. 2: 24 / *Extras*: 1Cor. 6: 12-20
    b. 1Cor. 9: 24-27 / *Extras*: Ge. 39: 6, 1Sa. 16: 12
    c. Phil. 4: 8
    d. 1Tim. 4: 8 / *Extras*: 2Tim. 3: 16

e. Mt. 22: 14 / *Extras*: Jonah 1: 1-3
f. Ro. 8: 35-39 / *Extras*: Gal 5: 6-15

Extras:
1Cor. 2: 6-16
Eph. 1: 3-14

CHAPTER TEN

The Call of God

The Call of God

REDEMPTION

Let's talk about God's plan of redemption.
(Bringing people back to God)*

God has thought about it long and hard to come up with the perfect plan.

Are you ready to hear this? (All must be broken)

Yes, every knee will bow and tongue Confess, that the lord is God almighty!

And if a person does not confess his or her sin and rebellion. That person will remain apart from God forever.*

<u>One must believe:</u>

• God is still on the throne and he is in control of heaven and earth.*

• Jesus was sent into the world to save sinners and he was resurrected back to the right hand of God to make intercession for those being saved.*

• Jesus resurrection is for the repentance and forgiveness of sins and proof of life after death.*

• The Holy Spirit is a promise of God from the very beginning. The Holy Spirit is here to lead you, guide you, convict you, comfort you, and lead you into all truth about the righteousness of God.*

Note: True worshipers are the kind of worshipers; God is looking for because they worship in spirit and truth. God is spirit and his worshipers must worship in spirit and in truth.*

The Call of God

Footnotes:
 a. Jn. 3: 16-17 / *Extras*: 2Cor. 5: 17-21
 b. Phil 2: 8-11 / *Extras*: Mt. 5: 23-24, 1Jn. 5: 16, 1Jn. 1: 9
 c. Ps. 47: 8 / *Extras*: Rev. 3: 21, Rev. 22: 1-6
 d. Lk. 5: 31-32
 e. Lk. 24: 44-47
 f. Ac. 1: 4-8 / *Extras*: Lk. 24: 48-49
 g. Jn. 4: 21-24

Extras: advice
 Young ladies – 1Tim. 5: 14-15
 Money – 1Tim. 6: 17-21
 Throne – Ps. 11: 4, Isa. 6: 1
 Jesus – Heb. 1: 1-14
 Holy spirit – 2 Pe. 1: 21, Heb. 2: 4, 2Th. 2: 13, Phil. 2: 1-9

Spirit & Truth:
 2Tim. 1: 12-14
 Ro. 8: 1-27
 2Cor. 1: 2-11
 2Tim. 2: 14-26
 2Tim. 4: 16
 1Th. 1: 5
 Jn. 16: 1-16
 Jn. 15: 26
 Jn. 14: 15-31

The Call of God

NEW COVENANT

God found fault with the first covenant and he established a new covenant the body of an individual. (A personal relationship)

God took it upon himself and he put his laws (words) in their hearts and on their minds. God has established himself as their God and they are his people, no longer will a man have to teach his neighbor or brother to know the lord because they will all know him from the least to the greatest!

God has promised to forgive their sin because God will teach them.*

(Your body is the temple of God)

So God starts drawing people to himself by spirit, miracles, signs, and wonders. (Divine intervention)*

Draw near to God and God will draw near to you!*

Footnotes:
    a. Heb. 8: 7-13 / *Extras*: Heb. 10: 5-18
    b. Jn. 6: 44-45 / *Extras*: Heb. 2: 4
    c. Jas. 4: 7-8 / *Extras*: 2Ch. 7: 14-22

The Call of God

MEN AFTER GOD'S OWN HEART

God has chosen, men after his own heart (men of God) to go out into the world to look for lost people. (Sheep)*

They (men of God) are to tell the lost people to return home, back to God in paradise with a repentant, remorseful, humble, and respectful attitude toward God.*

God is one who judges the thoughts and attitude of the heart. You can't fool God as you do some people. Like wise, you can't fool the one God sends to you because God has equipped the man of God for his Mission.*

Footnotes:
   a. Jn. 21: 15-17
   b. 2Cor. 5: 20-21 / *Extras*: Ez. Chapter 34
   c. Heb. 4: 12 / *Extras*: 2Tim. 3: 16-17

The Call of God

RUNNING FROM GOD

Now many are called, but few are chosen. And all have heard the word, but not everyone wants to hear the word of God. Because the word is offensive to many of them and a burden or a waste of time, that takes away from their own routine!*

The word of God tells us, that men or women are without excuse. The word will be preached and made known to the people of earth. (Nations)*

Footnotes:
    a. Jonah 1: 1-3 / *Extras*: Jer. 6: 10
    b. Ro. 1: 18-20 / *Extras*: Isa. 53: 1, Lk. 9: 60

CHAPTER ELEVEN

Salvation

Salvation

TURNING TO GOD

Since men and women are stubborn, hard-headed, or hard hearted. God sends his beloved son into the world to spread the message of hope to the lost and broken hearted.*

God sends Jesus to call sinners to repentance, so the sick can be healed from a broken spirit and a hardened heart toward God. (Bitterness)*

It's down to the now or never stage for the sinner and the sinner is close or near death at this point. Now God is making a last appeal to save the sinner from his or her own destruction.*

God allows the messenger to deliver the message of hope and redemption, so the sinner can be reconciled or restored to holiness.*

(True life) Life in God's presence again. This is called salvation. Salvation is found in Jesus because Jesus represents love for the lost and broken hearted.*

God loves Jesus and God loves you too!*

Footnotes:
   a. Jn. 1: 9-14
   b. Lk. 5: 32 / *Extras*: Heb, 3: 12
   c. 2Cor. 5: 20 / *Extras*: Ac. 2: 38-41
   d. Isa. 53: 1 / *Extras*: Heb. 3: 12-14
   e. 2Cor. 7: 10 / *Extras*: Lk. 24: 47, Ac. 20: 21, Ac. 26: 20, Ro. 2: 4, 2Pe. 3: 9
   f. Jn. 16: 26-27

PARABLE OF THE TENANTS

Now to prove what I'm saying, Remember the story Jesus told about the man who had a large vineyard. The man rented it out to some people and the time came to pay the owner for renting his vineyard. So the owner sent his servant to collect the debt owed, but the users said, (We will not pay) and bandit together to beat the servant.

So the owner sent another servant and they killed him too! The owner sent a third and got the same result. (Stoned to death)

Then the owner sent his son and the users said ah! The heir has come let us kill him and take his inheritance.

So now, that the truth has been revealed and the owner knows their heart or (intentions).

Finally the owner came and put an end to those wretched or evil men.

Footnotes:
 a. Mt. 21: 33-41

THE IMPORTANCE OF BELIEVING GOD'S WORD

We see God sent his servants into the world. God sent his son as a last appeal, then God will come and pass final judgment.

People who use others will end up with nothing not even their lives.

The users had an opportunity to make wealth; pay the owner, live at peace with God and man, but the devil filled their hearts with greed and disrespect.

The scriptures say; what is it to gain the whole world and lose your soul!*

God is always fair in every circumstance, but people don't pay attention to God. God gives us plenty of warnings, that is why we put him first (not last)!*

Footnotes:
    a. Lk. 9: 25
    b. 1Cor. 10: 6-11 / *Extras*: 2Ki. 1: 1-10

CHAPTER TWELVE

Spreading the Message

HISTORY

God was not unaware of Satan's schemes. God sent his son Jesus to tell the world about the greatest power on earth and in heaven. (Love!!)

God so loved the world, he gave his only begotten son, that who ever believes in him will not perish (be destroyed), but have eternal life.*

God warns us, that what ever we do should be done in the light and in his presence (for God and through God in Jesus name!*

The world did not want to hear the Son (Jesus) or the message of Love! So they hated Jesus without reason, and they killed him because they did not want their actions to be exposed.*

Footnotes:
    a. 2Cor.2: 11 / *Extras*: Eph: 6: 11
    b. Jn. 3: 16
    c. Jn. 3: 21
    d. Jn. 3: 19-20 / *Extras*: Jn 15: 25, Eph. 5: 11, 1Jn. 3: 4-12

PUTTING YOUR HOUSE IN ORDER

So all through out creation or history. God has chosen men to warn and save people with the same message.*

Repent for the kingdom of heaven is near, so turn around (straighten up)

And put your house in order.

If God had to put heaven in order (and we are made in his likeness) then we must put our house in order as it is in heaven.*

Footnotes:
    a. Isa. 53: 1
    b. 2Ki. 20: 1-7

PERSECUTION

These messengers from Abel down to Jesus have been righteous men, faithful, and loyal. These dedicated men of God risk their lives for the word of God and your salvation. (They were ridiculed, punished and killed.)*

Footnotes:
a. Lk. 11: 39-54 / *Extras*: Heb. 11: 1-40

EQUALITY

Jesus said, "There will be men who come after him, that will do greater things than he did!"*

There have been a few men, (we should mention) who risked there lives for righteous causes. Such as:

(The Disciples, Gandhi, Abraham Lincoln, Martin Luther King Jr., Nelson Mandela, and many more not mentioned.)

These great men deserve our applause, but it all happened because God loved the world and loved us first.*

Footnotes:
   a. Jn. 14: 12
   b. 1Jn. 4: 19

CHAPTER THIRTEEN

Trusting God

ENDURANCE

We truly owe thanks to Jesus, who set the wheels of endurance into motion. Jesus endured opposition from sinful or evil men to the point of death on the cross.*

Jesus resisted the Devil by the word of God and his testimony. He laid down his life to be totally used by God the Father.*

Footnotes:
    a. Heb. 12: 1-8 / *Extras*: 2Tim. 2: 3-12, 1Cor. 4: 12
    b. Rev. 12: 10-11 / *Extras*: Mt. 10: 22-28, Mt. 24: 9-14

SUBMISSION

We see, Jesus was not willing to take or settle for less, than what God desired for life.

(Meaning to live in Gods presence forever!)

Jesus was made a little lower than the angels to carry out his mission with faithfulness, loyalty, and diligence to the very end to bring God the Father (God almighty) the glory he deserves!*

Now Jesus is the author and finisher of our faith and Jesus has been seated at the right hand of God with angels, authority, and powers in submission to him.*

Footnotes:
    a. Heb. 2: 5-11
    b. Heb. 12: 2 / *Extras*: 1Pe. 3: 21-22

Trusting God

LOYALTY

Now we see not even the mightiest angel was able to do what Jesus did.

(To prove God's point)

God wanted us to understand the reason; he created man for himself.

(Man is God's glory)

Jesus did remain faithful in human form, that's how awesome God is my friends!

God already knew, what the devil was up to and created man to praise him!*

Remember Satan or Lucifer who use to be in charge of God's praises.*

Now I ask you again with tears in my eyes (as I write this).

• Why isn't the Devil serving God?

• More importantly, why do people even listen to him ?

The Devil is a liar, but Jesus deserves our full attention to the glory of God the Father amen!

Footnotes:
    a. Heb. 2: 3-11 / *Extras*: Jas. 1: 17-18
    b. Isa. 14: 12

GOD KEEPS HIS PROMISES

One: God raised Jesus from the dead.
        (Immortality / Eternity)

Two: God seated Jesus at his right side.
        (Glory and honor)

Three: God made Jesus an heir in heaven.
        (God prepared a place for him)

God has truly kept his word and promises. So we see, God is not a man, that he should lie or the son of man, that he should change his mind.*

Footnotes:
    a. Nu. 23: 19

CHARACTER

We should not lie to each other, but keep our word and not change our mind all the time (to be considered liars).

A double minded man is unstable in all his or her ways, that person will not receive anything from the lord.*

The resurrection is really the hope we believe in because God raised Jesus from the dead and God is able to raise us also (if we remain faithful until the end).*

There is nothing to hard for the lord. (God almighty)*

God truly loves his creation and God expects them to sincerely repent, when disciplined by God as children he delights in!*

Footnotes:
    a. Jas. 1: 5-8
    b. Heb. 2: 11-18
    c. Ge. 18: 13-15
    d. Lk. 24: 44-48 / *Extras*: Heb. 12: 5-8

CHAPTER FOURTEEN

Making a Change

NO EXCUSES

Now we see (once again) that people are without excuse. God loves them. So ask yourself right now, (why don't people love God?) Because you should!*

God is your best friend. God has promised never to leave you or forsake you and Jesus is a friend that sticks closer than a brother.*

Note: People leave God (they turn away from him).*

Footnotes:
   a. Ro.1: 20
   b. Dt. 31: 6 / *Extras*: Heb. 13: 5, Pr. 18: 24
   c. Heb. 3: 12

REMEMBERING WHAT GOD HAS DONE

Let us remember "Foot prints in the sand; during the roughest times of our life it was then, that God carried us through the storms of life."*

Please don't let go of Gods hand and don't give up!

(Let us walk with God as Jesus did)

Footnotes:
    a. Job 42: 10-16
    b. 1Jn. 2: 5-6

CHAPTER FIFTEEN

What About Love

What About Love

EXAMINING LOVE

For someone to truly understand, he or she must walk in love.

What is love?

(Good question) I thought you would never ask because after all the world gives you a different definition of love.

What About Love

WORLDLY LOVE

The world says, I love you as long as you pay the bills, take me out to have fun, provide for me, pay the car note, groceries, trips, clothes, and jewelry, but if you run out of money or material things.

Then I'm out of here, so long, see yah later, that's a sad way to live.

(That's spiritual death) a life apart from God.

This is the reason the divorce rate is so high. People have made money there God.

(Especially in America)

Let's face it; America has become the (great whore) in the bible. America has the highest divorce rate among nations.

American women are out of control with women's - lib. Women's - lib has under minded God's plan for perfect unity and union with God.*

America permits and promotes gay and lesbian marriages. America does not take care of its own citizens, but Americans are always in someone else's business.

(Country as well as individuals)

Americans are not busy at home, their busy playing games. (Pleasure)

America continues to play God in politics with countries and peoples lives.

The bible says: people listen to lies and they love it that way. (False hood)*

America keeps picking (electing) false leaders who rob the

country broke and lead them blindly into corruption.*

Jesus said; "All who came before me were thieves and robbers"*

Footnotes:
  a. 1Tim 2: 11-14 / *Extras*: 1Tim 3: 11, 1Tim 5: 13-15,
     Tit 2: 3-5
  b. Jn. 8: 42-47 / *Extras*: Tit 1: 10-16
  c. Mt. 15: 14 / *Extras*: Ac.2: 40, 1Cor. 15: 33-34, d. Jn. 10: 8

What About Love

THIS IS LOVE

(I think you get my point) Now this is love, not that we first loved God, but God first loved us and made a plan of salvation and redemption to draw us back to himself out of sin. God loved us even while we were still sinners.*

God is love because love comes from God. Who ever has been born again loves God and knows God.*

God's love is made complete in us, when we love one another. We need not fear because the man who walks in love is made perfect by obeying God's command.*

Footnotes:
   a. 1Jn. 4: 10, 19
   b. 1Jn. 4: 7-8
   c. 1Jn. 4: 16-18

What About Love

WALKING WITH GOD

So we see that walking with God. The man of God is able to Learn from God and relies on God (by faith) because he truly knows that God loves him.*

Then the man of God is capable of teaching and instructing his wife and they (as a couple) can show their children (the right example) of how to live and please God.*

You can not find this love, joy, and peace in any other life style, but in (Holy marriage).

It trains people to be loving, kind, forgiving, and able to work with one another for a common purpose (to please God not themselves).*

This creates unity and peace which transcend the true spirit of love. And this is love to walk in obedience to God's commands or principles.

Footnotes:
 a. 1Jn. 4: 16
 b. Eph. 5: 22-28 / *Extras*: 1Cor. 14: 35
 c. Gal. 5: 22-23
 d. 2 Jn. 1: 6

OBEYING THE COMMAND OF LOVE

As we obey Gods commands. We pass from death to life in Gods presence. Since the darkness is passing, we see the love of God shining as a bright light that gives hope to all who see it. This is to the Father's glory in Christ Jesus.*

Footnotes:
  a. 1Jn. 3: 14

What About Love

REFUSING TO WALK IN LOVE

What about the man who refuses to walk in love?

This person is a lost and restless soul that walks around in darkness because hate has blinded him.*

This person has been deceived by Satan because of his or her continual lust for the world (to be friends with it) in partnership with evil thoughts.*

This person's mind is unstable and reprobate because they can no longer distinguish good from evil. They hate because they do not know how to love and the person must repent and turn to God (who is love).*

Why you ask?

Well let's break it down, the word of God tells us with out love you can't gain anything as we seen earlier in the story of the vineyard. (Users)

So let us examine the characteristics of love very carefully and patiently.

• To love or not to love, that is the question?*

Footnotes:
    a. 1Jn. 4: 20
    b. 1Jn. 2: 15-17
    c. 1Tim 4: 1-5
    d. 1Cor. 13: 1-3

What About Love

THE MEANING OF LOVE

The word of God tells us, that love is patient and kind, it does not envy or boast and it's not proud. It is not rude, self seeking or easily angered. It keeps no record of wrongs. Love does not delight in evil, but rejoices with the truth. It always protects, always trusts, always hopes, and always perseveres. (Love never fails)*

This scripture tells us the very nature of God and the spirit of love. It tells us this divine nature is above worldly love.

One: Love tells us to go the extra mile with someone, especially our mate or spouse, and children, but also with one another.*

Two: Love tells us the type of attitude, we should be displaying toward one another.*

Three: Love tells us not to be like the Devil, who was kicked out of heaven for being rude, proud, and selfish with an at all cost mentally to get what he wanted.

(That's not love)*

Note: I did not say what he needed. The Devil was also easily angered.

(All borderlines of hatred)*

Fourth: The scriptures tell us not to judge one another, not to keep a running inventory of wrongs, but to forgive sin. (One sin at a time)*

Fifth: Love tells us to be in agreement with the truth and not to be happy with someone's down fall. Love warns us to be aware of such an attitude, So we don't fall next.*

Sixth: Love tells us to help preserve people and encourage one another daily.*

Seventh: Love tells us to endure hardship and walk as Jesus did. Love lets us know (if we endure in it) we will never fail in the sight of God and man!*

Footnotes:
  a. 1Cor. 13: 4-8
  b. Mt. 5: 40-42
  c. 1Jn. 3: 11-24
  d. Isa 14: 12 / *Extras*: Rev. 12: 7-9
  e. Gal 5: 19-20
  f. Mt. 7: 1-5
  g. Gal 6: 1, 10
  i. 2Pe.1: 3-11

WALKING IN LOVE

So there you have it brothers and sisters of the lord (as long as we walk in love).

We need not fear, but rejoice in the true spirit of God.*

If we refuse to walk in love, then we can be sure the eyes of the lord are watching us in the light or the darkness.*

We should not be like unreasonable children and lean to our on understanding.

Because the scripture says: "When I was a child, I talked like a child, I reasoned like a child, but when I became a man. I put childish ways behind me. (A man of God that is)*

I understand now these three remain; Faith, Hope, and Love, but the greatest of these is Love!*

Footnotes:
    a. 1Jn. 4: 18
    b. 1Pe. 3: 12
    c. 1Cor. 13: 11
    d. 1Cor. 13: 13

CHAPTER SIXTEEN

Overcoming

BORN AGAIN

So my friends, since God has shown us his great love. This love is found in the death, burial, and resurrection of his son Jesus Christ.

A person must be born again to enter the kingdom of heaven or see it. Since we understand, then we are baptized into the Father, the Son, and the Holy spirit of love.

And the three are in agreement together.

Also: The <u>water</u> (baptism), the <u>blood</u> (of Jesus), and the <u>Holy spirit</u> of (love and truth),

This testifies all are in agreement!

Footnotes:

    a. Jn 3: 16 / *Extras*: Lk 24: 45-48, 1Cor. 15: 20-28
    b. Jn. 3: 3-7 / *Extras*: Mt. 28: 5-10, 16-20
    c. 1Jn. 5: 6-8

Overcoming

HOLY SPIRIT

God has promised from the beginning to those who love him.*

(If they repent and are baptized)

They would receive the Holy Spirit. And this is how we know that he lives in us.

We know it by the spirit he (God) gave us.*

(The Spirit to Love)

Now let us walk in step with the spirit!

Footnotes:
    a. 1Cor. 2: 6-16
    b. 1Jn. 3: 24

Overcoming

THE GREATEST COMMANDS

We see God has given us a set of commands to follow:

One: Love God with all your heart, soul, mind, and strength. (First)*

Two: Love the family God gave you. (Spiritual home life)*

Three: And love your neighbors (God's creation)*

If we carry out God's commands, this will be love for God because his commands are not burdensome and everyone born of God overcomes the world.*

This will be our victory in the Lord, even our faith to overcome the world by the blood of Jesus (forgiveness) and our testimony. (Holding to the truth in love)*

Since everything has been said, simply believe it with the faith of a little child trusting in his or her parents.*

Do not add to it, do not take away from it or judgment will follow in Jesus name!

Footnotes:
   a. Mk. 12: 29-30
   b. Mt 12: 48-50 / *Extras*: Gal. 6: 10
   c. Mk 12: 31
   d. 1Jn. 5: 1-3
   e. 1Jn. 5: 4-5 / *Extras*: Jn. 16: 33
   f. Mt 18: 1-3
   g. Rev. 22: 18-21 / *Extras*: Ro 1: 18-32

Conclusion

Now that God has shown us his great love. Know nothing in all creation should be able to separate us from the love of God that is in Christ Jesus.

Now read (Romans 8: 29-39) as a command.

Since God first loved you, also love God and this is truly the end of the matter!

(Let no one deceive you)

May the grace and peace of God guard your hearts in Christ Jesus amen!

Scripture Index

Ex 19: 5-6
Dt. 4: 1-40
Dt. 6: 1-25
1Cor. 2: 6-16
1Cor. 7: 15-20, 39
1Cor. 9: 5-6
1Cor. 11: 7-12
1Cor. 13: 1-13
1Pe. 3: 1-22
2Pe. 1: 3-4
2Pe. 1: 19-21
1Tim. 2: 1-15
Lev. 19: 1-4
Mt. 28: 18-20
Ex. 19: 3-8
Ex. 31: 12-13
Jn. 3: 1-21
Jn. 4: 23-24
Act. 2: 40-41
Eph. 1; 5, 11
Ac. 2: 39
Mt. 12: 48-50
Ge. 1: 1-8
Ge. 12: 1-3
Ge. 2: 1-3
Ge. 1: 31
Ge. 13: 14-18
Ge. 26: 2-6

Lk. 6: 39-40
Ge. 2: 7
Ge. 2: 19
Ge. 2: 18-24
Ge. 2: 24
1Tim. 3: 1-15
Ge. 3: 17
1Tim. 2: 11-15
Eph. 6: 1-4
Col. 3: 20
1Tim. 4: 1-16
2Tim. 3: 16-17
Tit. 2: 1-15
Heb. 5 11-14
Heb. 12: 7-15
Ge. 2: 1-3
Rev. Ch. 12
Rev. 12: 7-8
Dan. 8: 15-19
Isa. 14: 12-23
Rev. 12: 3-4, 7-9
Jude 9
Dan. 10: 13, 21
Dan. 12: 1
Dan. 9: 20-23
Lk. 1: 11-20
Lk. 1: 26- 38
Job 1: 6

Job 1: 6
Dt. 30: 19-20
Rev. 12: 12
2Cor. 11: 14
Rev. 12: 9
2Cor. 2: 11
Eph. 6: 10-12
Ge. 3: 1
Mt. 4: 1-11
Ge. 3: 2-4
Hab. 2: 2-4
1Cor. 10: 1-13
Ps. 1: 3
Eph. 5: 22-28

Scripture Index

Ge. 28: 10-14

Ac. 3: 17-26

Ac. 17: 24-34

Ro. 4: 16-25

Eccl. 4: 12

Mt. 19: 4-6

Ge. 3: 9-13, 17

Ge. 2: 4-8

Ge. 2: 16-17

Ge. 15: 1

Pr. 22: 6

Ge. 1: 28

Phil. 4: 12

Heb. 11: 1

1Cor. 9: 24-27

Ge 17: 1-14

Heb. 4: 13

Ge. 3: 9

Rev. 12: 9

Ge. 3: 9-15

2 Sa. 12: 9-12

Ge. 3: 22-24

1 Cor. 10: 13

1Cor. 15: 58

1Cor. 16: 13

Isa. 54: 17

Ro. 8: 31

Ps. 34: 17-19

Zec. 3: 2

Mt. 16: 23

Pr. 15: 3

Rev. 12: 3,4,7,9

Rev. 12: 7-9

Mk. 4: 15

2Cor. 11: 14

Rev. 12: 9

Rev. 20: 2, 7

Dt. 17: 2-5

Dt. 17: 6-7

Dt. 17: 2-4

Rev. 12: 12

Rev. 12: 7-9, 12, 17

Isa. 14: 12-23

2Tim. 3: 1-5

2Tim. 3: 16

Mt. 22: 14

Jonah 1: 1-3

Ro. 8: 35-39

Gal. 5: 6-15

1Cor. 2: 6-16

Eph. 1: 3-14

Jn. 3: 16-17

2Cor. 5: 17-21

Phil. 2: 8-11

Mt. 5: 23-24

1Jn. 5: 16

1Cor. 11: 1-3

Ps. 1: 3

2Cor. 10: 3-8

1Cor. 8: 1

Ge. Ge.3: 6

Ge. 39: 6-12

Ge. 3: 17

1Ki. 11: 1-4, 7-9

Eph. 5: 22-24

Pr. 31: 1-3

1Pe. 3: 7

1Tim. 2: 14

2 Cor. 11: 3

Ge. 3: 11-13

Jer. 5: 1-3

Jer. 9: 3-9

Jer. 6: 10

Ro. 1: 18-20

Isa. 53: 1

Lk. 9: 60

Jn 1: 9-14

Lk. 5: 32

Heb. 3: 12

2Cor. 5: 20

Ac. 2: 38-41

Isa. 53: 1

Heb. 3: 12-14

2Cor. 7: 10

AND THIS IS LOVE: *A Spiritual Guide*

Scripture Index

Ps. 54: 7

Ac. 2: 21

Joel 2: 32

Ro. 10: 13

Isa. 53: 1

2Cor. 2: 14-17

2Cor. 2: 6-11

2Cor. 7: 8-13

Ac. 2: 39-41

2Cor. 7:1

Ge. 3: 17

Ge. 3: 13

Ge. 3: 16

Ge. 3: 15

Eph. 6: 12

Rev. 12: 4-7

2Cor. 6: 16-17

1Jn. 2: 15-17

2Cor. 6: 14-18

Phil. 4: 4-9

2 Pe 2: 4-10

2Pe. 2: 7-8

Ge. 39: 8-10

Jdg. 16: 16

1Jn. 4: 5-6

Pr. 3: 5-6

Ge. 39: 7-10

1Tim. 3: 12-13

1Jn. 1: 9

Ps. 47: 8

Rev. 3: 21

Rev. 22: 1-6

Lk. 5: 31-32

Lk. 24: 44-47

Ac. 1: 4-8

Lk. 24: 48-49

Jn. 4: 21-24

1Tim. 5: 14-15

1Tim. 6: 17-21

Ps. 11: 4

Isa. 6: 1

Heb. 1: 1-14

2Pe. 1: 21

Heb. 2: 4

2Th. 2: 13

Phil. 2: 1-9

2Tim. 1: 12-14

Ro. 8: 1-27

2Cor. 1: 2-11

2Tim. 2: 14-26

2Tim. 4: 16

1Th. 1: 5

Jn. 16: 1-16

Jn. 15: 26

Jn. 14: 15-31

Heb. 8: 7-13

Lk.24: 47

Ac. 20-21

Ac. 26: 20

Ro. 2: 4

2Pe. 3-9

Jn. 16: 26-27

Mt. 21: 33-41

Lk. 9: 25

1Cor. 10: 6-11

2Ki. 1: 1-10

2Cor. 2: 11

Eph. 6: 11

Jn. 3: 6

Jn. 3: 21

Jn. 3: 19-20

Jn. 15: 25

Eph. 5: 11

1Jn. 3: 4-12

Isa. 53:1

2Ki. 20: 1-7

Jn. 14: 12

1Jn. 4: 10

Heb. 12:1-8

2Tim. 3:-12

Jn. 21: 15-17

2Cor. 5: 20-21

Ez. Ch. 34

Heb. 4: 12

Scripture Index

Ge. 2: 24
1Cor. 6: 12-20
1Cor. 9: 24-27
Ge. 39: 61Sa. 16:12
Phil. 4: 8
1Tim. 4: 8
2Tim. 2: 3-12
1Cor. 4: 12
Rev. 12: 10-11
Mt. 10: 22-28
Mt. 24: 9-14
Heb. 2: 5-11
Heb. 12: 2
1Pe. 3: 21-22
Heb. 2: 3-11
Jas. 1: 17-18
Isa. 14: 12
Nu. 23: 19
Jas. 1: 5-8
Heb. 2: 11-18
Ge. 18: 13-15
Lk. 24: 44-48
Heb. 12: 5-8
Ro. 1: 20
Dt. 31: 6
Heb. 13: 5
Pr. 18: 24
Heb. 3: 12

Heb. 10: 5-18
Jn. 6: 44-45
Heb. 2: 4
Jas. 4: 7-8
2Ch. 7: 14-22
Jonah 1: 1-3
1Cor. 13: 4-8
Mt. 5: 40-42
1Jn. 3: 11-24
Isa. 14: 12
Rev. 12: 7-9
Gal. 5: 19-20
Mt. 7: 1-5
Gal. 6: 7-9
Mt. 7: 1-5
Gal. 6: 7-9
Gal. 6: 1, 10
2Pe. 1: 3-11
1Jn. 4: 18
1Pe. 3: 12
1Cor. 13: 11
1Cor. 13: 13
Jn. 3: 16
Lk. 24: 45-48
1Cor. 15: 20-28
Jn. 3: 3-7
Mt. 28: 5-10, 16-20
1Jn. 5: 6-8

2Tim. 3:16-17
Lk. 11: 39-54
Heb. 11: 1-40
Jn. 14: 12
1Jn. 4: 10
Heb. 12: 1-8

AND THIS IS LOVE: *A Spiritual Guide*

Scripture Index

Job 42: 10-16
1Jn. 2: 5-6
1Tim 2: 11-14
1Tim. 3: 11
1Tim. 5: 13-15
Tit. 2: 3-5
Jn. 8: 42-47
Tit. 1: 10-16
Mt. 15: 14
Ac. 2: 40
1Cor. 15: 33-34
1Jn. 4: 10, 19
1Jn. 4: 7-8
1Jn. 4: 16-18
1Jn. 4: 16
Eph. 5: 22-28
1Cor. 14: 35
Gal. 5: 22-23
2Jn. 1: 6
1Jn. 3: 14
1Jn. 4: 20
1Jn. 2: 15-17
1Tim 4: 1-5
1Cor. 13: 1-3

1Cor. 2: 6-16
1Jn. 3: 24
Mk. 12: 29-30
Mt. 13: 48-50
Gal. 6: 10
Mk 12: 31
1Jn. 5: 1-3
1Jn. 5: 4-5
Jn. 16: 33
Jn. 16: 33
Mt. 18: 1-3
Rev. 22: 18-21
Ro. 1: 18-32

About the Author

To: Whom it may concern
From: Voice of the People

We are writing because we have encountered an extraordinary individual on this planet in America. His name is John Dye (man of God) and he is just that, never have we met anyone who lives up to the name like this man sent by God.

This man has touched and helped, also healed the hearts and minds of so many people. You must meet him for yourself, and then you will know he is not from this world and that's a good thing. The Spirit of the Lord rest on him in a mighty way. He is truly anointed. He is a person that you can sense love flow from him to you. You can tell he is genuinely concerned about your affairs or problems and he is willing to help (not only help, but has the answer to all your questions about life).

Wise is an understatement to make about "Dr, Rev, Teacher, Minister, Counselor, John Dye (man of God)." He is so much more (a friend that sticks closer than a brother).

We have prayed and he has come our way to answer our prayers as well as fulfill the prayers of so many others. Thank God for sending John Dye into our lives and this world. We need him now more than ever in these terrible times.

So please allow this man to speak on television, so he can teach and reach the world. If you think the pope touched people wait until, they hear John Dye (man of God). Someone who has been in the spiritual, mental, emotional, and physical battle fighting for Gods people to deliver them from evil.

John Dye (man of God) should meet Oprah, Barbara Walters, 60 Minutes, 48 Hours, Talk shows, Time Magazine, and the President.

AND THIS IS LOVE: *A Spiritual Guide*

About the Author

There is no doubt in our mind, that this man deserves the" Noble peace prize" for all the hard work and lives he has touched for God!

We think you should do a major story on John Dye (man of God). You should give him a contract as a "Broadcast Minister and a Reality Show with a tour bus moving around the country helping people, or you should make him a strong Journalist for the Truth" during these false and terrible times.

John Dye (man of God) needs a National platform to speak from. John should meet all the "Leaders in this Country and the World." We believe this would be in every body's best interest to bring Truth and Peace to the world because (John is sent by God).

John Dye (man of God) can use all the supporters: Financially, Media Relations, Contacts, ect, that he can get to help him do the good. (God has called him to do)!

Thank you.

Voice of the people

Testimonies

John Dye is an Evangelist, Activist, Motivational speaker, and Spiritual counselor that is constantly in touch with the needs of the people in accordance with God's will and grace.

TESTIMONIES:

To Whom It May Concern:

I thank Brother John Dye, for his words and wisdom of our Father, Christ Jesus. Brother Dye has given me a better understanding of the Lord and the word of the Lord.

Brother Dye is a blessing of God. He has given me something more to look forward to as my life goes on in this world. When times are a little hard for me, I asked Brother Dye for advice, for words of wisdom and prayer, that everything will be okay.

I praise Brother Dye and give him thanks for being here and for helping those who want to hear the word of the Lord. So they too, can lead a more spiritual life/ so, in all who thank him for his blessing. I say, "Praise Brother Dye and thank him for all he has done." "In Jesus name" Amen.

Matthew L. Luthringer

To Whom It May Concern:

During my stay in the E.C.J, I have accepted Jesus as my savior. I got saved March 28, 2004. As I began studying the Bible, I found it hard to understand, (KJV) Then I met John Dye and was blessed for the way he explains the scriptures, and he encouraged me to get a N.I.V study Bible so I could have a better understanding on what I was reading.

Since we have started our Bible study in the mornings, John's wisdom has encouraged me to learn more and dig deeper into the pages of the Bible. John is the best preacher I have ever heard; he explains God's word so clear that I may understand it. John also has taught me not to worship earthly things in the flesh but to worship our God in heaven in everything I do.

I believe God put John in E.C.J. to teach, encourage and save some lives, and I am one of them. John has been an inspiration to me and others, I believe he is a blessing sent from above to help us all see the light. Not only has John helped me to understand the Bible better, but he also helped me to understand my purpose in life! Thank you John!

Yours Truly, Josh Parkins

To Whom It May Concern:

Brother John Dye! May you be blessed in life because you have been a true blessing to us all in ward #5. You have given us all a peace of mind and have encouraged us all to live the word of God. You've made a difference in our lives and the way we see it.

God sent us an angel and that's you my Brother. I would like to hear the word more from you on the street. My information will be with this. May God bless you and yours always.

Your brother, Drake Newton

HOW YOU CAN HELP!

If you would like to support this ministry and help get the
"Truth out in this World."

Please send all donations and gifts to:

Heart Ministries
Attn: Evangelist John Dye
P.O. Box 722
Mishawaka, Indiana 46546

Contact: (please send to both e-mails)
E-mail: revjohndye@comcast.net
E-mail: revjohndye@yahoo.com

Cell: (574) 220-3363

www.heartministriesonline.com

DID THIS BOOK HELP YOU!

If so please send your replies to Heart Ministries (Evangelist: John
Dye) and look for our DVDs, Tapes, and other Literature.

Please mail, call or log-on to get what you need for your
"Spiritual Growth."!

HEART MINISTRIES

DVDs / VHS tapes / CDs

1. Why worry.
2. God's way is higher.
3. Don't let sin keep you from God.
4. What's a famine?
5. Love with action and deeds not words.
6. Raising the standard.
7. Be careful what you listen too.
8. The truth will set you free.
9. Every body has a chance.
10. If you care

AND THIS IS LOVE: *A Spiritual Guide*

THANKS FOR YOUR SUPPORT!

DVD's / CD's continued

11. God is first not last
12. Suffering for good
13. Be sure
14. Blessings and Curses
15. There is one who knew
16. Opposites attract
17. Spiritual Warfare
18. A Tree and its Fruit
19. The Lords Prayer
20. The End

Heart Ministries really appreciates your support in helping us get out the "*Truth*" thru Book, DVD's and CD's.

I want you to know your contribution has not been in vain, but it has gone to changing the hearts, minds, and souls of the people in this world.

Bringing them to an understanding of; (The Way, the Truth, and the Life)

God predestined for us before time began (in Love)!

"Heart Ministries Supporters"

Patrick Motors: Salesman Terry (of Elkhart, IN.)
Budget Auto: Owner Dale & Salesman Lee (of Elkhart)
Complete Auto: Owner Michael (of Elkhart)Euro Auto Inc:
Owner Andrew (of Elkhart)
Patriot financial Inc: Gary (of Elkhart)
Worldwide Jewelry & Pawn: Owner (of Elkhart)
Blessings Instruments: Manager Randall (of Elkhart)
Maurice Trucking: Owner Maurice (of Elkhart)
Assistant: Minister Terry Hershberger (of Elkhart)
Assistant: Helper Courtney Draughter (of Berrien Springs, MI.)

God Bless you!
Sincerely
Rev. John Dye

Biography

(I knew, I was from God as a little child)

I was born in Gary, Indiana. My mother's name was Mary and she was from down south or (southern part of the United States). I never had a Dad; (God) is the only father, I ever knew. My mother moved me away from Gary, IN. as a baby to Elkhart, IN.

I would talk about God to my siblings and mother as a child growing up in our home, and then I moved with my uncle around the age of twelve. (Enjoying sports)

While in Elkhart, I attended Hawthorne Elementary and Pierre Moran Jr. High at these Schools, I won numerous Championships from fifth to the ninth grade in Football, Basketball, and Track. I went on to Central High School where I played in every Sectional Championship Basketball game for three years. The point is God was establishing me as a winner and leader from the very beginning. I was good at every thing, I put my hands too.

I attended Marian College in Indianapolis, IN. briefly for Basketball, but certain events brought me back to Elkhart. Then I realized the role Politics played in people's lives and how unfair or prejudice people could be toward each other.

Elkhart showed me the lowest level of life in every way imaginable morally, mentally, physically, and spiritually. The quality of people's lives was not good and the way they treated one another was even worse. The prejudice attitude was at an all time high (especially in work places) as well as social functions. You could see the division!

I observed selfishness and ignorance at its best through poverty, drug abuse, and alcoholism. Also hatred, discord and jealousy played major roles in people's destruction. It all stemmed from an economy that was divided. God showed all this to me (as he shaped and molded me) so that I would be able to save his people in the future.

In 1995 God appeared to me and talked with me to tell me my mission. God filled me with his spirit, wisdom, truth, love, and understanding (above all things).

"I am the man of God." Since then, God has up held my every word.

God Bless You
Evangelist John Dye